Political Campaign Communication

Political Campaign Communication

Principles and Practices

Updated Eighth Edition

Judith S. Trent, Robert V. Friedenberg,
and Robert E. Denton, Jr.

ROWMAN & LITTLEFIELD
Lanham • Boulder • New York • London

Published by Rowman & Littlefield
A wholly owned subsidiary of The Rowman & Littlefield Publishing Group, Inc.
4501 Forbes Boulevard, Suite 200, Lanham, Maryland 20706
www.rowman.com

Unit A, Whitacre Mews, 26-34 Stannary Street, London SE11 4AB

British Library Cataloguing in Publication Information Available

Library of Congress Cataloging-in-Publication Data

978-1 5381-1005-8 (paper)

♾TM The paper used in this publication meets the minimum requirements of
American National Standard for Information Sciences—Permanence of Paper
for Printed Library Materials, ANSI/NISO Z39.48-1992.

Printed in the United States of America

Political Campaign Communication in the 2016 Presidential Election

An Update to the Eighth Edition
of Political Campaign Communication
by Robert E. Denton, Jr.

Preface to the
Updated Eighth Edition

The 2016 presidential campaign was like none other in contemporary history. The campaigns for both candidates violated the norms, practices, and expectations of political pundits, journalists, and practitioners. The implications for future contests are still unknown. The historic nature of the contest in terms of gender, new communication technology and social media, the deep political divide in America, as well as the personalities of the candidates provided the environment for a very unique and untraditional campaign. Certainly, any course dealing with political campaigns must include the historic 2016 presidential election. Thus, we think it is important to provide an overview of some of the more important elements of political campaign communication for the election.

The additional chapter generally follows the precepts and outline of the eighth edition, especially part II: Practices of Political Campaign Communication. The chapter is segmented into distinct sections that may be easily incorporated in discussions and chapters from the text. Hopefully, the brief overviews of the topic areas will provide examples for discussion from the 2016 campaign.

The first introductory section provides a brief overview of the election results and raises some explanations for both its unique character and outcome. Sections "Candidate Surfacing Phase," "The Primaries," and "The Conventions" correspond to the areas discussed in chapter 2: Communicative Functions of Political Campaigns. The "Debates" section can be integrated into chapter 8: Debates in Political Campaigns. The section on "Advertising" provides detailed analysis of the strategies and tactics both campaigns utilized in their paid media efforts. This section blends with considerations from chapter 10: Advertising in Political Campaigns.

Of course, the use of social media and other new communication technologies became major factors of the campaign, especially with Donald Trump. The section on "Social Media" not only discusses the historic role of social media and the strategies and tactics of each campaign, but the section also provides an overview of the platforms of Twitter, reddit, Snapchat, Instagram, YouTube, and Facebook used by the campaigns. The material updates the information found in chapter 11: New Communication Technologies and Political Campaigns.

An equally significant consideration for the campaign was how journalists and the media covered the campaigns and the rise of what became known as "fake news." Some analysts argue we witnessed a transformation of journalistic practices in covering the election. The section on "Journalism and the 2016 Presidential Campaign" focuses on how the media covered the campaign, some of the issues that arose, and the influence of "fake news" in the coverage.

Finally, it is impossible to discuss the 2016 election without addressing the issue of gender. Not only was Hillary Clinton the first woman to be nominated for president by any party in American history, but also Donald Trump was caught up in several controversies related to gender. The challenges women face in political campaigns are well known in the literature. The section overview on "The Issue of Gender" considers comparisons between Clinton's run for the nomination in 2008 and 2016, how Trump managed the issue, and how both appealed to the women's vote. Perhaps most surprising is how "third wave" feminists and younger women responded to the Clinton campaign. This section serves as example across several chapters to include chapters 3, 8, and 9.

The ninth edition of the volume will update even more topics and areas related to the 2016 presidential campaign. It will include new chapters on the evolving role of the media in covering campaigns and ethics. Special attention will also be given to social media and new communication technologies. The following chapter will hopefully provide a bridge until the new edition is available.

Political Campaign Communication in the 2016 Presidential Election

Robert E. Denton Jr.

Scholars of presidential campaigns note that every campaign is unique and historic, especially in terms of candidates, issues, strategies, and elements of the strategic environment. However, to characterize the 2016 presidential election as historic is an understatement indeed. The election was certainly unique to the modern era of political campaigns. Many campaign conventions, norms, and expectations were thrown out the window. Scholars, pundits, and certainly veteran journalists were continually confounded by candidate performances, campaign events, and strategies. Without exaggeration, Donald Trump pulled off one of the greatest political feats in modern history. Pundits and scholars will continue to study and analyze this election in the coming years. Many argue that the impact of this campaign will not only impact elections of the future but also the nature of the contemporary practice of journalism and no less notions of participatory democracy.

On Election Day, Donald Trump put together the winning coalition of non-college-educated, working-class, and nonurban voters who turned out in record numbers.[1] Especially in critical Midwest battleground states, the disaffected wanted change. In the immediate aftermath of the election, there was the meme of Trump's victory based on hateful, racist, xenophobic, misogynistic, and homophobic attitudes of his supporters. Others made the assertion that the election was not based on issues; rather, it was based on personalities. Seldom have we had two candidates running for office with such high disapproval ratings and perceptions of ethical misgivings. Although some observers claim the election was not based on issues, however, I would offer some caution. Those voting for Trump, as revealed in exit polls, were indeed motivated to vote based upon issues:

- 56 percent of voters who saw the Supreme Court nominations as "the most important factor" supported Trump.
- 64 percent of voters who thought immigration was the "most important issue" voted for Trump, as did 86 percent of those who want a wall built on the U.S.-Mexico border.

1

- 83 percent of voters who felt Obamacare "went too far" supported Trump.
- 57 percent of those who viewed terrorism as the top issue backed Trump, as did 85 percent of those who thought the fight against ISIS was going "very badly."
- 73 percent of voters who felt the "government [is] doing too much" went for Trump.

Exit polls also revealed that the vast majority of voters expected Clinton to continue the policies of President Obama. For some, the election represented a referendum on the Obama administration; for others it was a rejection of establishment candidates, norms, and "business as usual."

After the election, the focus of discussion was equally on how Clinton lost what was a virtual certainty of election. Explanations included Clinton as a poor candidate, the campaign ignoring the Rust Belt battleground states, and FBI director James Comey's surprise announcement of reopening the private server investigation and the thousands of leaked emails from the campaign, to name only a few. In hindsight, tactical errors were noted of the Clinton campaign. In the end, although winning the popular vote the Clinton campaign underperformed among young people, minorities, and the white working class. She also underperformed in the thirteen swing states where Obama won rather easily, yet Trump won by 1.8 percent.[2] Finally, what we also learned is that voters deciding within the last week of the election went for Trump.

Another factor that must be noted is the 2016 presidential election was one of the most polarized elections in contemporary history along the lines of ideology, party, income, gender, and age. For more than a year prior to the election, national anger and frustration grew to historic levels. Polls revealed that the public was frustrated with the direction of the nation and with the institutions of government. Americans, especially those in the middle class, blue-collar workers, and minorities were downright angry. Not since the 1990s have we witnessed such general anger and political fragmentation. An argument can be made that the general frustration may well explain the candidacies of Donald Trump and Bernie Sanders.

As observers of campaigns, one could not help but note a rather dramatic shift in media coverage during the campaign in tone and aggressiveness. Trump's relationship with the media during and after the campaign may well have changed the nature of American political journalism.[3] Journalists were more aggressive, challenging, contextualizing, fact checking, and even editorializing more than in the past because of Trump's confrontational style and often sweeping generalizations, or even what some would label falsehoods. As a result, especially for Trump supporters, the "mainstream media" appeared biased, hostile, liberal, and as advocates for Clinton. More will be discussed on the transformative nature of media coverage and consequences of the 2016 presidential campaign later in this chapter.

The purpose of this chapter is to provide a brief overview and general summary of some of the variables of political campaign communication in the 2016 presidential campaign. Topic areas mirror many of those in the primary text, to include: candidate surfacing, the primaries, the conventions, the debates, advertising, social media, journalism and fake news, and issues of gender.

CANDIDATE SURFACING PHASE

According to Craig Allen Smith, Republicans and Democrats approached the primaries with very different issue concerns.[4] Republicans were very dissatisfied with government in general, followed by the economy and immigration. For Democrats, the primary concerns were the economy, unemployment, and gridlock in government. Polls also revealed major differences between the parties on issues of national security, the federal deficit, race relations, and terrorism, to name a few.[5]

Republicans started with seventeen candidates expressing interest and the Democrats with five. According to Smith, during the candidate-surfacing phase of a campaign, critical considerations include ability in fund-raising, obtaining major endorsements, the nature of media coverage, rankings in national polls, and success in the all-important Iowa caucuses.[6] Hillary Clinton clearly dominated the surfacing stage of the campaign, followed rather closely by Bernie Sanders. Among the Republicans, it was much more complicated, and various candidates had strengths and weaknesses across all the five elements of the surfacing phase of the campaign. The dominant candidates to emerge were Donald Trump, Marco Rubio, and Ted Cruz, while Jeb Bush, Ben Carson, and John Kasich committed to compete in the primary season.

THE PRIMARIES

Perhaps no candidate was better positioned to receive the nomination than Hillary Clinton. In addition to being the former First Lady, Clinton had served as senator from New York and secretary of state. Yet as the primary season began, many claimed that over the years she became one of the "elites," a multimillionaire with an elaborate lifestyle. She was a grandmother in her late sixties with rumors of health considerations. Bill Clinton's past followed her as she tried to appeal to a younger generation. Hillary had her own potential scandals, with questions of the Clinton Foundation and her use of a private server as secretary of state. For some Democrats, there was simply "Clinton fatigue," a time for new leadership, new ideas, and generational change.[7]

Although even older than Clinton, Bernie Sanders provided new and "progressive" ideas about issues, policy, and the role of government in American lives. A self-proclaimed Socialist and long-time independent, Sanders advocated for tax increases on the wealthy, greater government services across the board, and equally important, he voted against the Iraq war. He grew a following among the most liberal and younger members of the party. He appeared "authentic" and spoke with conviction. Throughout the early primary season, Sanders focused on the economy and political reform. While moving to the left as well, Clinton aggressively pursued the African American vote, embracing the Black Lives Matter movement. Clinton inched toward the nomination with major victories on Super Tuesday. Sanders's supporters vowed to continue to the convention. As Ceaser and his colleagues observe, "Bernie Sanders lost the nomination but won the party."[8] According to polls, Sanders enjoyed a higher favorability rating than Clinton.

Republicans had a wealth of promising potential candidates to select a nominee: governors, senators, business people, and even a noted surgeon. There was ethnic and ideological diversity represented among the contenders. Republicans controlled the federal House, Senate, and many state legislative bodies. Initially, few politicians, pundits, or political operatives took the candidacy of Donald Trump seriously. However, soon it became clear that he was developing a devoted following. To many, he tapped into their anger and frustration. Many Republican primary voters liked his boldness, aggressiveness, and "tell it like it is" approach to issues. They especially liked his attacks upon the media, Washington culture, and the call for change across the board. Other candidates found it difficult to gain free airtime, as Trump dominated the news cycle. Media attacks as well as those of opponents during debates actually backfired, providing motivation for stronger support among Trump devotees. One by one, Trump prevailed in the primaries. No controversy or attack slowed his momentum. Although splitting the vote in the primaries among the contenders, Trump won the Republican vote. Ceasar and his colleagues attribute his success because "he jumped out to an early lead, consolidated it while his opponents were busy fighting among themselves, and held on despite late advances by others."[9] In the end, Trump won twenty-seven of the forty-two state contests. Although victorious, as the conventions approached Trump's task was to unite the party and provide a rationale for his candidacy.

For the primaries, Republicans enjoyed a record number of primary voters and the second highest number of primary voters for the Democrats.[10] In total, more than sixty million citizens participated in the presidential primaries. Part of the reason is 2016 was the first election in eight years without an incumbent. There was high interest in both parties. In addition, the two high-profile and historic candidates of Hillary Clinton and Donald Trump clearly added excitement and "drama" to the nomination process.

On the Republican side, Trump dominated the media coverage, receiving over $2 billion in "free media" coverage. As a candidate, he moved from less than 5 percent support among Republicans to more than 30 percent support by the beginning of primary voting.[11] Trump dominated the primaries, winning seventeen of the twenty-one primaries. Bernie Sanders in the Democrat nomination race enjoyed enthusiastic supporters; however, Hillary Clinton dominated the two-person race, receiving four million more votes and commitments from the "super delegates" heading for the convention. According to Rhodes Cook, the turnout profiles of the primary season did provide clues to the pending fall election. The Trump campaign brought in new Republican voters across key demographic groups. In addition, his campaign outperformed Democrat rivals in key battleground states such as Florida, Iowa, Michigan, North Carolina, Ohio, and Wisconsin. Thus, according to Cook, Trump's success in these battleground states served as a harbinger for the fall election.[12]

THE CONVENTIONS

Given the nature of the primaries on both sides, there was much interest and excitement in anticipation for the party conventions. There were widespread expectations of drama, especially with the Republicans. Nominating conventions serve as the transition from the primary campaign to the general election. From a communication perspective, conventions "reaffirm and celebrate the democratic selection of candidates, thereby legitimizing both the process and the nominees. The conventions also create a communicative moment through which the political parties set aside the divisions evident in the primary campaign and establish party unity, commitment, and excitement for the general election. Finally, the conventions afford the candidate a platform to introduce and elaborate campaign issues and messages in a highly controlled, choreographed, and scripted production."[13] The parties create a narrative of American core beliefs, attitudes, and values. They share a vision of the nation and the path forward.

In the aftermath of the primaries, the national mood was still one of frustration and anxiety for the future direction of the country. In addition, both parties confronted internal splits within party loyalists. On the Republican side, there was speculation of a possible "brokered" convention. For Democrats, the challenge was to reassure Sanders's wing of the party that Clinton would honor some of his campaign's issue positions and causes. As Rachel Holloway notes, "Both candidates faced significant rhetorical challenges as they prepared for the nominating conventions."[14]

The Republicans

The Republican convention was first, and the theme was the now infamous "Make America Great Again." Each evening had a subtheme: Monday was "Make America Safe Again," Tuesday "Make America Work Again," Wednesday "Make America First Again," and Thursday "Make America One Again." Some opponents would not attend, nor former presidents George H. W. Bush or George W. Bush, nor former nominees John McCain nor Mitt Romney as well as numerous elected House representatives and senators. From an operational perspective, the convention lacked clear organization and campaign messaging. To make matters more difficult, there was a floor fight led by the "Never Trump" leaders to avert Trump's nomination. Collectively, Republican speakers presented a dangerous world—America under attack both internationally and domestically, all the result of the "Obama/Clinton" years in office.[15]

Members of Trump's family attempted to portray a "softer" image of Trump. Trump's wife, Melania, shared her story as an immigrant to this country and spoke at length of Trump's positive personal attributes of "caring," "fairness," and "kindness." While a very good effort, she was criticized for passages of similarity to Michelle Obama's 2008 Democratic Convention address. His son, Donald Trump Jr., spoke of his father's business successes and commitment to blue-collar workers. Eric Trump followed suit and detailed how his father would bring jobs and better health care for working families.[16]

Some of Trump's opponents did speak in support of Trump: Chris Christie, Ben Carson, Scott Walker, Marco Rubio, and Rick Perry. However, all eyes were on Ted Cruz. While allowed to speak, he had not provided any indication of endorsement. Cruz focused on conservative values and his agenda for the country. In the middle of his address, Trump entered the convention center with cameras focused. Cruz concluded with a call for action but did not formally endorse Trump. Cruz left the stage with resounding chorus of "boos."[17] Vice presidential nominee Mike Pence provided a more traditional address, articulating Republican values, a conservative agenda, and the rationale for supporting Trump. There were a diverse group of speakers in favor of Trump, mostly focusing on his personal values and agenda. Daughter Ivanka Trump introduced her father, characterizing him as an "outsider," "fighter," person of "compassion," and that he hires the best people for jobs. In essence, her father was simply the best person for the job and task of "Making America Great Again."[18]

Trump's acceptance speech was more than an hour, and according to Jim Kuypers, Trump's acceptance speech conformed to the general norms and expectations of a nomination acceptance speech.[19] The nation was in "crisis." Trump provided a litany of domestic and international problems. To change America required a drastic change in leadership. As an outsider, he alone could fix the economy, strengthen our position in the world, tackle terrorism and destroy ISIS, and protect our borders. Trump concluded:

> I am your voice. So, to every parent who dreams for their child, and every child who dreams for their future, I say these words to you tonight: I am with you, and I will fight for you, and I will win for you! To all Americans tonight, in all our cities and towns, I make this promise: We will make America strong again! We will make America proud again! We will make America safe again! And we will make America great again![20]

The Democrats

As with the Republicans, there was a last-minute effort by Sanders's diehard supporters to challenge Clinton's nomination on the floor of the convention. To make matters worse, just days before the convention over twenty thousand Democratic National Committee emails were released showing clear bias in favor of Clinton's nomination. This resulted in a change of leadership at the DNC. Despite protests, it was clear that Clinton would proceed to win the nomination.

The theme of the Democratic Convention was "Stronger Together." According to Holloway, unlike the Republican convention the Democratic Convention was well-organized, scripted, and choreographed with targeted messages and crafted videos that praised Clinton's achievements and future promises.[21] Every message was counter to Trump's statements, character, issue positions, and prescribed policies, often using clips of his own words during the primary campaign. Each evening hosted a diverse group of speakers and testimonials praising Clinton and attacking Trump. The first night featured speeches by Michelle Obama and Elizabeth Warren, with a video tribute to Bernie Sanders, who took to the podium to endorse Clinton. The message was one of recognizing the life work of Clinton in public service and party unity. On the second night, it was Sanders who made a motion to accept Clinton's nomination by acclamation.[22]

Throughout the convention, speakers included celebrities, noted political leaders, and representatives from key special interest groups and organizations such as Planned Parenthood Federation of America and the Mothers of the Movement from Blacks Lives Matter. There were speakers representing every major voting block, to include military veterans who could attest to her fitness as potential commander in chief.[23] The keynote speaker for the convention was former president Bill Clinton. As expected, he provided a firsthand account of their life together and her many fine attributes. Interestingly, he directly addressed the notion that she was an ultimate insider, who had been around too long on the political scene. He acknowledged:

> So, people say, well, we need to change. She's been around a long time, she sure has, and she's sure been worth every single year she's put into making people's lives better. I can tell you this. If you were sitting where I'm sitting and you heard what I have heard at every dinner conversation, every lunch conversation, on every long walk, you would say this woman has never been satisfied with the status quo in anything. She always wants to move the ball forward. That is just who she is.[24]

Other notable speakers included Vice President Joe Biden and President Barack Obama, as well as vice presidential nominee Tim Kaine.[25] Like Trump, Clinton relied upon her daughter, Chelsea Clinton, to share the more personal side of her role as mother and lessons learned in the face of crisis and defeat. Her mother was a "champion," "fighter," and "hero."[26]

In Clinton's acceptance speech, she contrasted her vision of America with the negative one of Trump. She portrayed Trump as polarizing, divisive, and the wrong temperament for the presidency. Clinton provided in great detail how she would address economic, social, and foreign policy issues.[27]

For Jim Kuypers, both campaigns achieved the goals of an acceptance address. "Both closed their respective primary contests; both lauded their respective political parties; both transitioned their respective campaigns to the general election. Certainly, both candidates attacked the opposition and acclaimed their own positions and parties."[28] However, from the public perspective, the Democratic Convention was more successful than the Republican Convention. More democrats were "more favorable" toward Clinton's candidacy in the aftermath of the convention.[29] There was a clear difference in tone and vision between the two conventions. However, both conventions acknowledged the anger and frustration of Americans across the board. And both conventions offered a candidate who would be a change agent. As Holloway observes, "Both candidates were described as pragmatic problem solvers who would 'have the back' of those who were forgotten or left behind. Both parties promised a leader who recognized and valued the 'common person.' Both campaigns promised to restore the American Dream, to focus on building a country that would benefit all Americans, especially those who felt the government no longer worked to support their well-being. Both candidates said creating a better world for future generations was a primary motivation of their campaigns."[30] In the end, Holloway argues that the nominating conventions actually "reaffirmed a deep concern among the American people, distrust in government."[31] As a result, neither candidate received a significant "convention bounce" in the polls, and both "entered the general election only slightly better off than when the convention began."[32]

THE DEBATES

As the general campaign began, both candidates had among the lowest approval ratings in contemporary history of presidential campaigns, both well under 50 percent. There was great anticipation for the pending debates between Trump and Clinton. Indeed, over eighty-one million tuned in to the first debate, establishing a historical record of viewers. The average audience across the three debates surpassed seventy-three million. Collectively, polls reveal that the debates were an "important factor" for 82 percent of voters. Historically, research shows that 7 percent of undecided voters select candidate preference based upon debate performance.[33]

According to Ben Voth, even the primary debates generated historic audiences, especially among the Republicans.[34] The first primary debate actually provided the first time the general public could witness Trump in exchanges with opponents and not in a "protected" environment like on the campaign trail. The first primary debate also provided a glimpse of how Trump would handle adversarial questions and personal attacks. The main headlines following the first debate focused on Trump with his attack on moderator Megyn Kelly and his refusal to take the pledge to support the winner of the nomination process. Republicans engaged in a total of eleven debates. With each debate, the field of candidates declined and Trump became less defensive and more focused on message and issues. However, he was the target of opponents and moderators.[35]

Each of the debates with Clinton provided "high drama" and key moments of exchanges that generated headlines and material for campaigns and pundits alike. While there is not space to provide a detailed synopsis of the debates, Ben Voth noticed several interesting findings from his analyses:

- During the debate period, Trump received historic negative media coverage in tone compared to generally favorable coverage for Clinton.
- Interestingly, both Trump and Clinton received about equal amounts of speaking time across the debates (moderators consumed about 15 percent of all speaking times).
- There were several noted incidents of collusion between the Clinton campaign and the moderators. Donna Brazile of CNN leaked questions to Clinton's campaign prior to one primary debate, and Matt Lauer deferred to Clinton's request not to ask a question about the then email scandal.
- Moderators became more active in the debates, playing the role of "fact checker," especially in terms of Trump. Moderators challenged, corrected, and interrupted Trump during the debates 106 times compared to Clinton's 44 times. In fact, moderators took 50 percent more time during the debates than in 2012. Thus, not only did we witness a new degree of activism by the moderators, they clearly focused on Trump more than Clinton.
- Despite the viewership and "rough and tumble" nature of the debates, neither candidate received huge bumps in the polls. There is some evidence that Trump might have benefited slightly from the exchanges.[36]

Polls did indicate that Clinton "won" the three debates, although each contained some "magic moments" of exchanges. However, the third debate was Trump's best in terms of overall performance. He showed more discipline, stayed on his message points, and was effective in challenging and attacking Clinton.[37] In the end, the debates did not appear to generate major shifts of support between the candidates. Trump met expectations of "being Trump," and moderators were criticized for being biased toward Clinton. However, the debate performances reinforced commitment to the individual candidates.

ADVERTISING

According to Scott Dunn and John Tedesco, political advertising is a candidate-controlled medium that allows campaigns to present positive messages about their candidates as well as to attack issue stances, opponent images, or to respond to the attacks made by the opposition. Most specifically, television advertising is a form of communication that allows candidates to create and disseminate messages without journalistic gatekeeping or direct interpretation.[38] Research shows that political advertising reinforces attitudes of base voters and may well sway low-information voters. As with virtually every other feature or characteristic of the 2016 presidential campaign, television advertising was also unique and historic. Televised spending and the total number of ads were down from the previous campaign. During the general campaign season, there were 117,000 ads aired compared to 256,000 during the 2012 presidential campaign.[39] Because Trump received so much "free media," he stated, "You know, I go around, I make speeches. I talk to reporters. I don't even need commercials, if you want to know the truth."[40] In terms of outside interests or "Super PAC" ads, over $1.5 billion was spent during the presidential campaign, up from about $1 billion in 2012. Three times more of the allocation was spent in favor of Clinton instead of Trump. Compare these numbers to $338 million in 2008.[41]

Overall, Dunn and Tedesco found that the ads in 2016 were primarily negative and image focused, with few ads focused on issues. Both candidates tended to rely upon comparative ads to convince the public that the candidate of the sponsorship of the ad was the least objectionable candidate alternative.[42] Lynn Vavreck found that 75 percent of Clinton's appeals in ads were about character traits, with only 9 percent focusing on jobs and the economy.[43] Clinton ads attempted to argue that Trump was clearly unfit for office primarily because of his temperament and lack of experience. Any positive Clinton ads focused on her record working for families and children. Clinton used several strategies in her ads. The predominant one was using Trump's own words from campaign events and media interviews to demonstrate his unfitness for office. His language, characterizations of immigrants and opponents, impersonations, and references to specific individuals such as Senator McCain and grandiose boasts portrayed Trump as a bad role model, bully, and bigot. A second strategy was to use anti-Trump quotes and comments by Republicans from well-known leaders such as Mitt Romney to testimonials from ordinary citizens. Finally, as mentioned above, the Clinton campaign used comparative ads to contrast Trump's lack of experience and questions of temperament compared to her "proven" qualities of leadership, experience, and empathy.[44]

The Trump campaign relied even more heavily on negative and comparative ads. The primary strategy for Trump's ads were focused on allegations of Clinton's corruption that clearly would make her unfit to be president. Most of the ads focused on words from FBI director James Comey, the many revelations from the leaked emails, and Clinton's contradictory statements about the email server. Ads also raised questions about Clinton's "fortitude, strength, or stamina." As with the Clinton campaign, the Trump campaign also used the strategy of using Clinton's own words to question her veracity and judgment. They especially put her comments characterizing Trump supporters as "the basket of deplorables" to good use. The campaign also used comparative ads to attack Clinton. In addition, several ads compared the differing visions of America between the candidates and Trump's experience in the private sector versus Clinton's experience in government. Collectively, the Trump campaign ads portrayed Clinton as a corrupt career politician.[45] Interestingly, about a third of Trump's appeal in ads was focused on economic issues of jobs, taxes, and trade.[46]

As will be discussed next, there were other media outlets for message dissemination. However, in terms of television advertising, the messages were highly negative, attempting to get people to vote "against" the other candidate rather than "for" either of them. As Dunn and Tedesco conclude from their analysis of the ads, "More ambivalent voters would have had a hard time discerning any compelling reason to vote for either candidate based on the campaign advertising (although they would have found plenty of reason to vote *against* both candidates)."[47]

SOCIAL MEDIA

Social media, broadly defined, has transformed electoral politics, especially at the national level. In fact, John Allen Hendricks and Dan Schill argue that "political campaigns today *are* social media campaigns."[48] Social media, of course, allows candidates to speak directly, without filter to voters. And the access is staggering. According to the Pew Research Center, 86 percent of Americans use the Internet, and among those, 80 percent use Facebook, 32 percent Instagram, 31 percent Pinterest, and 24 percent Twitter.[49] In addition, 75 percent of Americans own a smartphone.[50] During the 2016 campaign, 65 percent of voters sought news of the campaign from digital sources.[51] For Hendricks and Schill, the unprecedented use of social media in the 2016 presidential campaign led to unpredictability, disruption, and the blurring of political discourse.[52] Tweets would generate headlines, some Facebook posts would advocate "hate" and "violence," and rumors and dubious posts were treated as factual and accurate journalism. Often during the campaign, according to Diana Owen, "Social media fed the cable news media beast and drowned out legacy news journalism."[53]

For campaigns, social media provides two primary functions. First, social media campaigns can solidify and activate the candidate's base or core constituencies. Second, as discovered during the 2016 election, the use of social media can drive media coverage and stories of the campaigns.[54] The Clinton campaign used digital outlets to focus on solidifying her base targeted to women, young voters, and minorities. In contrast, Trump would use social media to attack opponents as well as the press, generating content that dominated news coverage almost on a daily basis.

These innovations to campaign communication, for good or bad, naturally fit Donald Trump. He saw the value of personal appeals and access to very distinct groups and voters without filters. Clinton's use of social media was to create "warm and fuzzy" images or as a key element of get-out-the-vote efforts. Trump, in contrast, used social media for highly personal statements, immediate reactions, and personal engagement with supporters.[55]

In terms of numbers, Trump enjoyed twenty-two million followers on his Facebook, Twitter, Instagram, and reddit accounts compared to Clinton's fourteen million. It is worthy to note that these numbers far surpass the daily viewership on cable network news outlets, to include leader Fox News.[56] The networks and cable outlets simply could not keep up or muster the audience, hence the influence of social media. The success of Trump on social media was, as noted above, one reason the Trump campaign spent so little and found little need to spend large sums of money on paid advertising. In fact, campaign social media generated $3.4 million in free media coverage for Trump and only $1.4 million for the Clinton campaign.[57]

The Clinton campaign had a staff of over one hundred assigned to its digital team responsible for all the content development, production, and execution of posts and advertising.[58] As already noted, the team wanted content to be highly favorable to Clinton and inspirational. The goal was to humanize Clinton with references to her roles as mother, wife, and grandparent. Clinton's podcasts attempted to make her more personable and open. And the Clinton campaign also used social media to attack Trump. The analysis of political communication scholar Jennifer Stromer-Galley found that the Clinton campaign posted three times more messages on issues than the Trump campaign. They also tended to provide facts backing any claims. In contrast, Trump used more personal posts with broad generalizations or more generic claims with little factual evidence.[59]

For the Trump campaign, son-in-law Jared Kushner led the social media efforts as well as the general campaign advertising strategy. Hendricks and Schill note that the campaign also relied heavily on "big data" to make message content and targeting decisions. The information also identified which issues and messages to target for different regions of the nation. Interestingly, the data also influenced decisions of travel, fund-raising, and speech topics.[60]

When considering platforms, Twitter was the dominant medium of choice for Trump. He also enjoyed the most "likes" and "retweets" during the campaign. Trump and/or his campaign tweeted more than three thousand tweets, with some estimates that one in eight were personal insults.[61] By Election Day, Trump had over thirteen million followers compared to Clinton's ten million. In addition, Trump supporters were most likely to "retweet," thus extending his reach and influence with potential voters.[62]

Although only 4 percent of Americans use reddit, the social media outlet that allows users to vote on content, 70 percent of users get news from the site. Users are younger and males. On this platform, Bernie Sanders was the most discussed candidate with comments (165,000), followed by Clinton (85,000) and Trump (73,000).[63]

Snapchat, a relatively new platform, was also popular among younger Americans eighteen to thirty-four. This medium provided the opportunity to reach the younger and millennial youth. Pictures and story content disappear after twenty-four hours. Users would post items from live campaign events. The postings were spontaneous and informal. Both Trump and Clinton purchased Snap Ads, ten-second videos that would capture an event, location, or "fun" moment.[64]

Both campaigns also used Instagram on a major scale. Trump had 1,300 posts with 4.5 million followers compared to Clinton with 835 posts with 4.2 million followers. Both campaigns shared personal stories, pictures of family, and informal shots at campaign rallies. Hendricks and Schill note that Trump actually broke campaign norms during the primaries by posting attack-style videos. These videos were also posted on other platforms.[65]

YouTube was a major source of campaign material. Over four billion views of candidate videos occurred in the last eight months of the campaign, well over one billion in the final month.[66] Both campaigns were virtually equal in usage and viewership. The ads were most effective, with three ranking among YouTube's top ten most watched ads in its history.[67] According to Hendricks and Schill, in addition to more traditional ads the most common videos were late-night comedy clips, commentary videos, news clips, debate exchanges, live events, and parody clips.[68]

Finally, Facebook was not only an essential part of the social media campaign for Trump and Clinton, political action committees and special interest groups used it as well. The platform even solicited campaigns offering special tools and capabilities.[69] The data collected on users of the platform allowed campaigns to "pinpoint individual voters at the most granular of levels and tailor messages to voters based on the issues and appeals that will be most likely to resonate with each individual voter."[70] On this platform, Trump, once again, led in followers with 12.2 million to Clinton's 8.2 million. For Trump, the Facebook appeals generated over $250 million in contributions. The Trump campaign also significantly utilized the Facebook Live function more than the Clinton campaign. On all aspects of Facebook, the Trump campaign dominated.[71]

JOURNALISM AND THE 2016 PRESIDENTIAL CAMPAIGN

Beyond the stories of the candidacy of Hillary Clinton, the victory of Donald Trump, and the unprecedented role of social media in 2016 is the impact and transformation of American journalism. Noted media scholar Diana Owen characterizes the 2016 presidential campaign as the demarcation of "the era of post-truth news." Alarming to Owen is the fact that press legitimacy was "being challenged by an alternative media universe where Twitter rants and fake news hijack the political agenda obscuring the important issues of the day."[72] While many acknowledge that Trump, with his countless tweets and campaign rally comments, provided plenty of fodder for criticism by the media covering the campaign, many individuals believed the media in general turned his remarks into a very negative caricature of him and thus of his supporters. In many supporters' minds, the media characterizations became personal. For example, some argued the media should not characterize Black Lives Matter supporters by extremist members, nor should the same occur for Trump supporters.

In an unprecedented action, the *New York Times*'s executive editor, Dean Baquet, and publisher Arthur Sulzberger printed a postelection letter vowing to "rededicate ourselves to the fundamental mission of *Times* journalism. That is to report to America and the world honestly, without fear or favor, striving always to understand and reflect all political perspectives and life experiences." However, they also claimed that their coverage was accurate and fair.[73]

Just after the election, Jim Rutenberg of the *New York Times* characterized the Trump victory as "a Dewey defeats Truman lesson for the digital age."[74] He noted that "the news media by and large missed what was happening all around it, and it was the story of a lifetime. The numbers weren't just a poor guide for election night—they were an off-ramp away from what was actually happening."[75] For him, the missed prediction of a Trump victory was more than an error in polling. "It was a failure to capture the boiling anger of a large portion of the American electorate that feels left behind by a selective recovery, betrayed by trade deals that they see as threats to their jobs, and disrespected by establishment Washington, Wall Street, and the mainstream media."[76] Rutenberg concludes that the election made "clear that something was fundamentally broken in journalism, which has been unable to keep up with the antiestablishment mood that is turning the world upside down."[77] However, Will Rahn of CBS News was less charitable. "We were all tacitly or explicitly #WithHer, which has led to a certain anguish in the face of Donald Trump's victory. More than that and more importantly, we also missed the story, after having spent months mocking the people who had a better sense of what was going on. . . . This is all symptomatic of modern journalism's great moral and intellectual failing: its unbearable smugness."[78]

As typical in recent presidential contests, the horse race between the candidates dominated the coverage, consisting of 42 percent followed by scandals and controversies with 17 percent and only 10 percent focusing on policy issues.[79] According to the Tyndall Report, the three major evening news networks devoted just thirty-two minutes to issue coverage in the 2016 general election. For ABC, the issue was terrorism for eight minutes; for NBC issues of terrorism, LBGT issues, and foreign policy for eight minutes; and CBS the issues of foreign policy, terrorism, immigration, policing, and the Environmental Protection Agency for a total of sixteen minutes. In previous presidential elections, coverage surpassed two hundred minutes. However, during the primary season, the networks spent 333 minutes focusing on Donald Trump. Clinton's emails garnered one hundred minutes of coverage from the networks.[80]

Overall, both candidates received highly negative coverage, with 66 percent for Clinton and a record-high 77 percent for Trump. Even when issues were discussed, 84 percent of the coverage criticized candidate positions. During the general campaign, Trump received 15 percent more coverage than Clinton, mostly of outrageous or provocative statements or behaviors at rallies. In addition, Trump surrogates received more airtime than Clinton surrogates.[81]

Trump was given a huge amount of time on the cable networks. They would cover his rallies in full. The networks also allowed him to phone in his interviews. This allowed him to hit multiple shows within minutes, flooding the airwaves, and he could avoid questions he did not like or provide glib answers. Even unedited, he got by with misleading statements, or what some would call actual falsehoods, without interruption or clarification.[82] In addition, according to Owen, cable news coverage of the campaigns provided hours of panels of highly partisan commentators who argued over every tweet and single lines from speeches uttered at rallies while largely ignoring more substantive issues and policies. "In-depth reporting was supplanted by a steady flow of sensational factoids, many of which were derived from candidates' and their surrogates' communications. To suit their format, cable news organizations repackaged legacy journalists' detailed analyses as superficial 'breaking news' snippets devoid of context or factual nuances."[83]

Matt Gertz actually argues that although the coverage became increasingly negative for Trump, the media was holding a rather low bar for his campaign, believing the public would not favor his candidacy. Thus most, if not all, of the media did not practice deep investigative reporting. There was no need, after all; most in the media openly questioned how folks could fall for Trump as president. Gertz concludes, "Editors and executives at major media outlets failed in their responsibility to present to their audience the full picture of the election in proper context, instead providing disproportionate scrutiny to relatively minor Clinton 'scandals' in a way that ultimately resulted in a skewed picture of the election."[84] In the end, "The political press was unable to adapt its methods and practices to a dramatically different election season."[85]

This election generated a new phrase: *fake news*. According to Owen, one of the hallmarks of the 2016 campaign was "the amount of misinformation, misleading stories, and bold-faced lies that were propagated."[86] Ceasar and colleagues view fake news as "deliberately falsified or distorted online stories that go viral within political communities of the left and right."[87] The preponderance of misinformation originated on social media platforms. Items "liked," "shared," and "retweeted" generated the "fake news" phenomena.[88] Highly partisan websites published questionable material of speculation, rumors, and innuendos. Websites would release fabricated, half-truth, speculative, and sensational stories that would sometimes be reported by cable and other journalists. Many of the sites, such as Infowars, The Rightest, or National Report, were designed to look like legitimate news sites or political blogs.[89] These websites received money based upon "hits," thus the more sensational the stories the more "hits" for the sites. The stories and material were "true" enough to appeal to the readers fitting their ideological and political preferences. The so-called fake news reached millions of people during the campaign. And the "fake news" was reposted and mentioned on legitimate sites such as Facebook or Snapchat and others. Examples of "fake news" widely reported include: Pope Francis had endorsed Trump, Clinton had sold weapons to ISIS, an FBI agent was found dead after participating in leaking Clinton emails, protesters at Trump rallies were being paid thousands by the Clinton campaign, Clinton was at the center of a pedophilia ring linked to Anthony

Weiner's (husband of Clinton's close aide Hume Abedin) alleged inappropriate emails to a minor, to name just a few.[90]

Social media encourages a "minute by minute" coverage of the campaign. Social media sources also exaggerate the sensational, the unusual, and the wacky relative to more traditional coverage of issues and events. Social media coverage seldom encourages the in-depth coverage and analysis of traditional media. Likewise, Ceaser and his colleagues argue today's new media environment creates echo chambers with outlets catering to narrow and specific political parties, ideologies, or issue perspectives. Facebook has algorithms that provide news stories that complement the political views of the reader.[91] Political discussions and exposure are with sources of "like mind." Thus individual beliefs, values, and prejudices are reinforced and seldom challenged. They argue that this environment allowed for the growth of "fake news," and report a survey where virtually 90 percent of both Clinton and Trump supporters believed conspiracies involving the other candidate basically at face value.[92]

According to Dartmouth political scientist Brendan Nyhan, this was "the most consequential election for political journalism in my lifetime."[93] For Nyhan, if "truth" is the standard, then a more aggressive approach, as noted at the beginning of this chapter, was well justified. However, it appeared that news organizations were more open and comfortable with expressing biases. Rich Lowry, editor of *National Review*, believes "going forward news organizations may become less apologetic about those biases. It could be a step to a British-style journalism that's a little more partisan and wears its biases on its sleeve."[94] Ron Schiller, former NPR chief, argues, "There's a newfound toughness, a pugilist form that reporters have been embracing."[95] Yes, Trump was the catalyst for this shift. However, the question is whether or not it is here to stay. Certainly, in the early stages of the Trump presidency, it appears to be the case.

THE ISSUE OF GENDER

According to virtually all political observers and pundits, Hillary Clinton was going to be elected the first woman president of the United States. Despite the surprisingly challenging primary season, the election was hers to lose. As noted in the introduction, it was Trump who managed a historic election upset. In the aftermath of the election, women voted in overwhelming numbers for Clinton; however, non-college-educated women voted for Trump two to one, and he won evangelical white women by double digits. Exit polls also revealed that many women who voted for Clinton did so with some ambivalence. Younger, "third wave feminists" stayed home compared to previous elections.[96]

There was no question that gender would be an issue in the presidential campaign, not unlike it was in the 2008 contest with the nomination fight between Obama and Clinton and with Sarah Palin as the Republican vice presidential candidate. There is a great deal of research that recognizes many challenges for women in American electoral politics, ranging from feminine versus masculine traits, level of perceived aggressiveness, management skills, role of emotion, and even dress, to name a few. During the campaign, as anticipated, there were some "gendered" issues raised about Clinton: comments about her hairstyles, dress pants, and fashion choices, shrill voice, and her shouting and screaming her lines at rallies.[97] A Rasmussen poll in 2016 reported that 78 percent of men and 79 percent of women could vote for a woman for president, but only 4 percent would vote for a woman *because* the candidate was female.[98]

Unlike the 2008 campaign where Clinton downplayed her gender and the historic nature of the potential of a woman president, in 2016 she used her gender as a strategic appeal. In terms of women, Clinton was quick to note the historic importance of the election of a woman president. Second, she reminded voters of her "feminist" credentials, and finally she addressed issues and positions most important to women voters, such as education, health care, gun control, equal pay, women's choice, and more. An interesting tactic that evolved was Clinton talking about her role as mother and now grandmother. Such discussions and appeals allowed her be perceived as more personable and warm.[99]

What became apparent during the primary season was that younger, millennial women were not enamored with her candidacy and felt no obligation to support Clinton because of her gender. The younger women viewed Clinton's feminism as more traditional, outdated, and limited. She lacked concerns of women of color, lower socioeconomic class, and issues of social and economic justice. To this generation of feminists, her appeal was more concerned with women empowerment. In addition, many younger women questioned her authenticity as a feminist because her entire career was based on her husband, Bill Clinton.[100]

To make matters worse, as the younger women became familiar with the Monica Lewinsky scandal, they questioned her comments and treatments of women who came forward accusing Bill Clinton of sexual assault. Of course, Trump entered the debate accusing Clinton of being a hypocrite in terms of defending her husband. According to him, she was actually "an enabler."[101] Any time the Clinton campaign would call Trump a sexist, supporters of Trump would claim she was using the "woman's card." Throughout the campaign, Clinton did try to appeal to millennials, relying upon surrogates such as actress Lena Dunham (creator and star of HBO's *Girls*) and singer Demi Lovato, who would introduce her at rallies.[102]

Issues of gender were actually equal or more central to the Trump campaign. During the primary period, Trump made headlines with attacks on former FOX anchor Megyn Kelly, opponent Carly Fiorina, and Ted Cruz's wife. In addition, he vowed to "punish" women who have abortions if they are made illegal and defended his campaign manager, who was accused of shoving a female reporter. During the primary season, Clinton enjoyed a twenty-point advantage over Trump with women voters. Among Republican women, he garnered half of their support. For those women who did support him, they largely discounted criticisms saying he was not politically correct, not a professional politician, and that he treats men and women equally and even hires more women in his companies than men. The "gender gap" problem followed Trump throughout the primary season.[103]

The myriad issues of gender, broadly defined, continued during the general campaign season. Gender, as a topic and related issues, dominated media coverage and political commentary, and also was addressed by the candidates. The

2016 presidential election evolved as the most "gendered" presidential campaign in American history. For Clinton, it was because she occupied a historic moment. However, for Trump, some argued he made gender an issue strategically and by design. Judi Sedivy argued that Trump proudly displayed his masculinity. He continually displayed his "maleness" in statements and actions.[104] At rallies, Trump encouraged the chant "lock her up," and that she didn't have a "presidential look" or the needed "stamina" to do the job. He raised questions of her health and state of mind.

The debates also displayed issues of gender both directly and indirectly. Trump was accused of "chauvinistic bullying" during the debates. For example, in the first debate, Trump had a total of seventy-three interruptions, to include seizing the floor from Clinton three times. Clinton only had five interruptions throughout the debate.[105] During the debate there was a "magic moment" when Clinton directly attacked Trump for his treatment of women by using the example of former Miss Universe Alicia Machado, who he called "Ms. Piggy" and "Ms. Housekeeping." For several days after the debate, Trump had to defend his comments and others considered demeaning toward women. Trump defenders noted his lack of direct attack on Clinton in response during the debate, that Clinton took money from countries that stoned and imprisoned women, and that she was a "phony feminist" for defending the behavior of her husband, Bill Clinton.[106]

Of course, one cannot discuss gender and the campaign without noting the *Access Hollywood* tape where Trump was very crass and even suggested an act of sexual assault. Trump apologized and described the exchange as "locker room" talk. General outrage was expressed universally, but among Republican women, 73 percent indicated they would still support him. The rationale was that issues and candidate positions were more important in the election.[107]

In response to the "gender gap," Trump hired Kellyanne Conway, a longtime Republican strategist and pollster. At all rallies Trump reiterated his love, support, and respect for women and addressed women's issues and concerns directly. Conway is credited with softening his rhetoric, keeping him more focused and disciplined in terms of messaging. She also encouraged his appeal to black voters to demonstrate he was not a bigot. In addition, Conway was a great media spokesperson for Trump. As a successful woman and mother of four small children, she could attack Clinton and demonstrate she understood the issues of concern for all women.[108]

In the final weeks of the campaign, both candidates made overt appeals to the women's vote. The Clinton campaign made several ads targeted to women using Trump's own words to reflect his "true" attitudes toward women and related issues. The Trump campaign used ads featuring his daughter Ivanka, a mother of three children herself, calling for laws to help women in the workplace. The Trump campaign emphasized the issues of health and education more than the Clinton campaign, especially in the final days.[109]

The "gender gap" in voting emerged in the 1980s. Married white women and white evangelical women favored Republicans, whereas minority and younger women favored Democrats. The "gap" went from the low double digits by the mid-1980s to the low twenties by 2000 forward. Many pundits predicted a record high in the size of the "gender gap" for 2016.[110] However, that would not be the case. Clinton received 54 percent to Trump's 42 percent of the women's vote. Upon further analysis, Trump received 53 percent of the white women's vote, 62 percent of white noncollege women's vote, 45 percent of white college graduate women's vote, and 89 percent of Republican women's vote. In fact, Clinton got 1 percent less of the women's vote than Barack Obama in 2012.[111] In the end, Trump performed as most contemporary Republican presidential candidates. Perhaps issues and life experiences mean more than gender when it comes to voting. Certainly, in terms of gender, identity politics did not play the role anticipated by the Clinton campaign.

Issues of gender were certainly an important part of the 2016 presidential campaign for both Clinton and Trump. No doubt women in record numbers voted against Trump, and those who voted for Clinton reveal some degree of misgiving. There were the expected gender characterizations and portrayals that hamper most women candidates for any office. However, it was unexpected reactions of the "third wave" feminist and younger women voters who largely rejected the notion of a first woman president as justification for voting for Clinton. In addition, who would have guessed the multitude of questionable sexist statements and behaviors of Trump in a presidential campaign? In her concession speech, Clinton did hold out hope and optimism that indeed a woman would become president sooner rather than later. "And to all the women, and especially the young women, who put their faith in this campaign and in me, I want you to know that nothing has made me prouder than to be your champion. Now, I know we have still not shattered that highest and hardest glass ceiling, but some day someone will and hopefully sooner than we might think right now."[112]

CONCLUSION

As noted in the introduction to this chapter, thousands of volumes and millions of pages will be written about the 2016 presidential campaign. Discussions about the 2020 campaign have already begun. Concerns about the role of the media continue, and it has become clear that Trump will be our first "Twitter President." And issues of gender will continue to be of concern, with several women's names being mentioned running for the presidency in four years. While traditional elements of campaign communication were evident and played major roles in the election, newer elements of social media and journalistic practices transformed the political campaign landscape in America.

Campaigns, as noted in the preface of *Political Campaign Communication: Principles and Practice*, are indeed a communication phenomena. They represent in many ways our national conversations on issues, policies, and government. Campaigns are also highly complex and sophisticated communication events. This chapter provided a very brief overview of some of the communication elements, strategies, and tactics of the 2016 presidential campaign.

NOTES

1. Much of this discussion is based on introductory material in Robert E. Denton Jr., "Preface," in *The 2016 US Presidential Campaign: Political Communication and Practice*, ed. Robert E. Denton Jr., vii–x (Cham, Switzerland: Palgrave Macmillan, 2017).

2. "56 Interesting Facts about the 2016 Election," The Cook Political Report, December 16, 2012, http://cookpolitical.com/story/10201, retrieved December 20, 2016.

3. Dylan Byers, "How Donald Trump Changed Political Journalism," Money.CNN .com, November 2, 2016, http://money.cnn.com/2016/11/01/media/political-journalism -2016/index.html?iid=Lead, retrieved November 15, 2016.

4. Craig Allen Smith, "Setting the Stage: Three Dimensions of Surfacing for 2016," in *The 2016 US Presidential Campaign: Political Communication and Practice*, ed. Robert E. Denton Jr., 3–25 (Cham, Switzerland: Palgrave Macmillan, 2017).

5. Ibid., 12–13.

6. Ibid., 15–20.

7. James Ceaser, Andrew E. Busch, and John J. Pitney Jr., *Defying the Odds: The 2016 Elections and American Politics* (Lanham, MD: Rowman & Littlefield, 2017), 43–46.

8. Ibid., 59.

9. Ibid., 94.

10. Rhodes Cook, "Presidential Primaries: A Hit at the Ballot Box," in *Trumped: The 2016 Election That Broke All the Rules*, eds. Larry Sabato, Kyle Kondik, and Geoffrey Skelley, 83 (Lanham, MD: Rowman & Littlefield, 2017).

11. Ibid., 85.

12. Ibid., 90.

13. Judith Trent, Robert Friedenberg, and Robert E. Denton Jr., *Political Campaign Communication: Principles and Practices*, 8th edition (Lanham, MD: Rowman & Littlefield, 2016), 34–45.

14. Rachel L. Holloway, "Midnight in America: The Political Conventions in 2016," in *The 2016 US Presidential Campaign: Political Communication and Practice*, ed. Robert E. Denton Jr., 30 (Cham, Switzerland: Palgrave Macmillan, 2017).

15. Ibid., 30–33.

16. Ibid., 34–37.

17. Ibid., 38.

18. Ibid., 41–44.

19. Jim A. Kuypers, "The Presidential Nomination Acceptance Speeches of Donald J. Trump and Hillary Clinton," in *Political Campaign Communication: Theory, Method, and Practice*, ed. Robert E. Denton Jr., 143 (Lanham, MD: Rowman & Littlefield, 2017).

20. "Donald Trump, Republican Presidential Candidate, Delivers Remarks at the 2016 Republican National Convention," *Federal News Service*, July 21, 2016, retrieved Lexis/ Nexis Academic database, June 16, 2017.

21. Holloway, "Midnight in America," 48.

22. Ibid., 48–49.

23. Ibid., 52–53.

24. "Bill Clinton Delivers Remarks at the 2016 Democratic National Convention," *Federal News Service*, July 26, 2016, retrieved from Lexis/Nexis Academic database, June 16, 2017.

25. Holloway, "Midnight in America," 54–58.

26. Ibid., 61–62.

27. Ibid., 61–64.

28. Kuypers, "The Presidential Nomination Acceptance Speeches of Donald J. Trump and Hillary Clinton," 161–62.

29. Holloway, "Midnight in America," 64.

30. Ibid., 65.

31. Ibid., 66.

32. Ibid., 67.

33. Ben Voth, "The Presidential Debates 2016," in *The 2016 US Presidential Campaign: Political Communication and Practice*, ed. Robert E. Denton Jr., 78–79 (Cham, Switzerland: Palgrave Macmillan, 2017).

34. Ibid., 81.

35. Ibid., 81–82.

36. Ibid., 80–94.

37. Ceaser et al., *Defying the Odds*, 112.

38. Scott Dunn and John C. Tedesco, "Political Advertising in the 2016 Presidential Election," in *The 2016 US Presidential Campaign: Political Communication and Practice*, ed. Robert E. Denton Jr., 99–100 (Cham, Switzerland: Palgrave Macmillan, 2017).

39. Ibid., 100.

40. Ibid., 100.

41. Michael E. Toner and Karen E. Trainer, "The $7 Billion Election," in *Trumped: The 2016 Election That Broke All the Rules*, eds. Larry J. Sabato, Kyle Kondik, and Geoffrey Skelley, 186 (Lanham, MD: Rowman & Littlefield, 2017).

42. Dunn and Tedesco, "Political Advertising in the 2016 Presidential Election," 108.

43. Lynn Vavreck, "Why This Election Was Not about the Issues," *New York Times*, November 23, 2016, https://www.nytimes.com/2016/11/23/upshot/this-election-was-not-about-the-issues-blame-the-candidates.html, retrieved June 22, 2017.

44. Dunn and Tedesco, "Political Advertising in the 2016 Presidential Election," 103–10.

45. Ibid., 110–15.

46. Vavreck, "Why This Election Was Not about the Issues."

47. Dunn and Tedesco, "Political Advertising in the 2016 Presidential Election," 115.

48. John Allen Hendricks and Dan Schill, "The Social Media Election of 2016," in *The 2016 US Presidential Campaign: Political Communication and Practice*, ed. Robert E. Denton Jr. (Cham, Switzerland: Palgrave Macmillan, 2017).

49. Shannon Greenwood, Andrew Perrin, and Maeve Duggan, "Social Media Update 2016: Facebook Usage and Engagement Is on the Rise, While Adoption of Other Platforms Holds Steady," *Pew Research Center*, November 11, 2016, http://pewrsr.ch/2fiOTBE.

50. Keely Lockhart, "Watch: Why Social Media Is Donald Trump's Most Powerful Weapon," *The [London] Telegraph*, September 22, 2016, http://www.telegraph.co.uk/news/2016/09/22/watch-why-social-media-is-donald-trumps-most-powerful-weapon/.

51. Diana Owen, "Twitter Rants, Press Bashing, and Fake News," in *Trumped: The 2016 Election That Broke All the Rules*, eds. Larry J. Sabato, Kyle Kondik, and Geoffrey Skelley, 172 (Lanham, MD: Rowman & Littlefield, 2017).

52. Hendricks and Schill, "The Social Media Election of 2016," 122.

53. Owen, "Twitter Rants, Press Bashing, and Fake News," 167.

54. Ibid., 173.

55. Hendricks and Schill, "The Social Media Election of 2016," 122–23.

56. Ibid., 124.

57. Darren Samuelsohn, "Trump's Twitter Army: New Data Show the GOP Nominee's Followers Are Exactly What the Dems Hoped they Weren't—Reliable Voters," *Politico*, June 15, 2016, http://politi.co/24QmtOC.

58. Hendricks and Schill, "The Social Media Election of 2016," 125–29.

59. Jennifer Stromer-Galley, "In the Age of Social Media, Voters Still Need Journalists," *U.S. Election Analysis 2016*, http://www.electionanalysis2016.us/us-election-analysis-2016/section-6-internet/in-the-age-of-social-media-voters-still-need-journalists/.

60. Hendricks and Schill, "The Social Media Election of 2016," 129.

61. Ibid., 134.

62. Ibid., 131.

63. Ibid., 136.

64. Ibid., 137.

65. Ibid., 139.

66. Ibid., 138.

67. Ibid., 138.

68. Ibid., 138.

69. Ibid., 140.

70. Ibid., 140.

71. Ibid., 141.

72. Owen, "Twitter Rants, Press Bashing, and Fake News," 177.

73. Liz Spayd, "One Thing Voters Agree On: Better Campaign Coverage Was Needed," *New York Times*, November 19, 2016, https://www.nytimes.com/2016/11/20/public-editor/one-thing-voters-agree-on-better-campaign-coverage-was-needed.html, retrieved May 24, 2017.

74. Jim Rutenberg, "A 'Dewey Defeats Truman' Lesson for the Digital Age," *New York Times*, November 9, 2016, https://www.nytimes.com/2016/11/09/business/media/media-trump-clinton.html, retrieved March 2, 2017.

75. Ibid.

76. Ibid.

77. Ibid.

78. Will Rahn, "Commentary: The Unbearable Smugness of the Press," CBS News, November 10, 2016, http://www.cbsnews.com/news/commentary-the-unbearable-smugness-of-the-press-presidential-election-2016/, retrieved February 2, 2017.

79. Owen, "Twitter Rants, Press Bashing, and Fake News," 169.

80. "Study Confirms Network Evening Newscasts Have Abandoned Policy Coverage for 2016 Campaign," Media Matters, https://www.mediamatters.org/print/739016, retrieved May 24, 2017.

81. Owen, "Twitter Rants, Press Bashing, and Fake News," 170.

82. Matt Gertz, "Election Post-Mortem: How 2016 Broke Political Journalism," The National Memo, December 30, 2016, http://www.nationalmemo.com/2016-broke-political-journalism/, retrieved February 2, 2017.

83. Owen, "Twitter Rants, Press Bashing, and Fake News," 169.

84. Gertz, "Election Post-Mortem."

85. Ibid.

86. Owen, "Twitter Rants, Press Bashing, and Fake News," 175.

87. Ceasar et al., *Defying the Odds*, 23.

88. Hendricks and Schill, "The Social Media Election of 2016," 130–31.

89. Owen, "Twitter Rants, Press Bashing, and Fake News," 176.

90. Ibid., 176–77.

91. Ceasar et al., *Defying the Odds*, 179.

92. Ibid., 23.

93. Dylan Byers, "How Donald Trump Changed Political Journalism," Money.CNN.com, November 2, 2016, http://money.cnn.com/2016/11/01/media/political-journalism-2016/index.html?iid=Lead, retrieved November 15, 2016.

94. Ibid.

95. Ibid.

96. Robert E. Denton Jr., "Issues of Gender in the 2016 Presidential Campaign," in *The 2016 US Presidential Campaign: Political Communication and Practice*, ed. Robert E. Denton Jr., 179–80 (Cham, Switzerland: Palgrave Macmillan, 2017).

97. See Ibid., 180–81.

98. "Should Women Vote First for Women?" Rasmussen Reports, February 11, 2016, http://www.rasmussenreports.com/public_content/politics/general_politics/february_2016/should_women_vote_first_for_women, retrieved July 2, 2017.

99. Denton, "Issues of Gender in the 2016 Presidential Campaign," 182.

100. Ibid., 182–84.

101. Amy Chozick, "'90s Scandals Threaten to Erode Hillary Clinton's Strength with Women," *New York Times*, January 20, 2016, http://www.nytimes.com/2016/01/21/us/politics/90s-scandals-threaten-to-erode-hillary-clintons-strength-with-women.html?_r=0, retrieved January 20, 2016.

102. Denton, "Issues of Gender in the 2016 Presidential Campaign," 184.

103. Ibid., 189–90.

104. Julie Sedivy, "Donald Trump Talks Like a Woman," POLITICO Magazine, October 25, 2016, http://www.politico.com/magazine/story/2016/10/trump-feminine-speaking-style-214391, retrieved October 26, 2016.

105. Ben Schreckinger and Daniel Strauss, "Did Trump Come Off as Sexist?" *Politico*, September 27, 2016, http://www.politico.com/story/2016/09/trump-women-sexism-debate-clinton-228759?lo=ap_e2, retrieved September 27, 2016.

106. Ibid.

107. Clare Malone, "For Many GOP Women, Party Loyalty Trumps Personal Affront," FiveThirtyEight.com, October 14, 2016, http://fivethirtyeight.com/features/for-many-gop-women-party-loyalty-trumps-personal-affront/, retrieved October 15, 2016.

108. Ibid.

109. Philip Rucker, "Trump Has a Challenge with White Women: 'You Just Want to Smack Him,'" *Washington Post*, October 1, 2016, https://www.washingtonpost.com/politics/trump-has-a-challenge-wit...ck-him/2016/10/01/df08f9ee-875b-11e6-a3ef-f35afb41797f_story.html, retrieved October 2, 2016.

110. Geoffrey Skelley, "Venus vs. Mars: A Record-Setting Gender Gap?" Sabato's Crystal Ball, July 7, 2016, http://www.centerforpolitics.org/crystalball/articles/venus-vs-mars-a-record-setting-gender-gap/, retrieved July 13, 2016.

111. Susan Page, "For Clinton, Sisterhood Is Powerful—and Trump Helps," *USA Today*, July 11, 2016, http://www.usatoday.com/story/news/politics/elections/2016/07/10/hillary-clinton-women-voters/86793244/, retrieved July 12, 2016.

112. "Hillary Clinton's Concession Speech (full text)," CNN, November 9, 2016, http://www.cnn.com/2016/11/09/politics/hillary-clinton-concession-speech/, accessed November 9, 2016.